THE SIMPLICITY OF LIFE

Other Books by Sheri A. Sutton

And So It Is

The Light of Christmas

In Remembrance of Me

Memorable Moments

40 Days

Songs of Faith and Hope

The One Called Jesus

The Simplicity of Life

Sheri A. Sutton

THE SIMPLICITY OF LIFE

© Sheri A. Sutton 2025

ISBN: 978-0-9984548-6-3

All rights reserved. Without limiting the rights under copyright reserved above, no part of this publication may be reproduced, stored in a retrieval system, or transmitted, in any form or by any means (electronic, mechanical, photocopying, recording. or otherwise), without the prior written permission of the copyright owner of this book.

Sheri A. Sutton
2 Callie Ct.
Wichita Falls, Texas 76310
United States of America
www.sheriasutton.com

I find relief in the soothing sway of the tree swing.

Sweet Summer Night, page 31

TABLE OF CONTENTS

Acknowledgments	ix
Preface	xi

Poems
Fall Comes Quietly	3
Holy Moment	4
Phenomenon	5
Another Winter Day	6
The First Winter Snow	7
Haiku	8
Christmas Eve	9
A New Year	10
Blank Pages	11
Haiku	12
Birth of Spring	13
Haiku	14
The Promise of Spring	15
Lady Redbud and Her Four Daughters	16
Song of the Mockingbird	17
Life's Good	18
Take Flight	19
Awaken	21
The Child Within	22
Thank You	23
Baby	24
Displaced	25
A Dog's Day	26
Texas Summer	28
Heat Wave	29
Rebirth	30

Sweet Summer Night	31
Haiku	32
Genuine Love	33

Closing Thoughts
    Writer's Choice … 35

About the Author … 37

ACKNOWLEDGMENTS

With sincere gratitude to my dear friend and fellow poet, Geneva Rodgers, for her editorial review.

Certain poems in this book have been previously published in the following:

A Celebration of Poetry
Memorable Moments
Poetry Society of Texas *A Book of the Year*

PREFACE

For fifteen years, my husband and I lived on a property of 160 acres that included farmland and a variety of trees such as evergreen, cottonwood, hackberry, mesquite, and pecan. The Wichita River ran south along the eastern property line and then dog-legged west. Along the river, there were approximately two miles of trails that we frequently walked and explored. Close to the trail was a sweet grove of pecan trees that we used for picnics. On the north side of the property was our homestead which also included two barns and pastures for our two horses.

It was a beautiful place to live and enjoy with family and friends as we visited over dinners, gathered for reunions and birthdays, and celebrated many holidays. Wonderful memories were made that I cherish still today.

During our time on this property, I was moved to write the poems in this book. These poems, however, are not about farm life. Instead, these poems are my impressions of what I witnessed and experienced around me — the simplicity of life.

We live in such a hectic and chaotic world. More often than not we don't take time to breathe, to sit in silence, and to witness the simple things of life that bring laughter, joy, and tears.

These poems capture a few of those simple things I experienced including a baby rabbit, a super moon, a thank you note from my granddaughter, and a winter snow. I believe that it is in the simplest things of life, like the sway of a tree swing, that we receive the greatest blessings — blessings that continue to put a smile on our face, tears in our eyes, and joy in our heart.

May this book of simple things experienced in my life bring a blessing to your life.

Sheri A. Sutton

POEMS

Fall Comes Quietly

Days grow short, morning dew glistens on grass blades;
landscape color pallet fades slowly into autumn.
Birds in formation begin journey to warmer climates
as Monarch butterflies, a beautiful fall surprise,
visit briefly before continuing southern migration.

> Fall comes quietly,
> October winds blow gently —
> leaves rustle all day.

Simple picnic lunch savored as I watch sunbeams
from western sky dance through pecan trees.
Sunlight warms body and soul. Hammock swings
and tenderly rocks my sleepy spirit.

Sadly, weekend respite ends. Healing peacefulness is broken
as fallen leaves crackle beneath my footsteps.

> Evening sun sets now —
> colors of red, orange, pink
> stretch across the sky.

Crisp evening air, promising winter's approach,
requires jacket for warmth. Brilliant stars
illuminate dark infinite vastness of night sky.
Harvest moon teases my empty hammock.

I smile. In the weeks ahead, I will revisit
the memories of today.

Holy Moment

Lush green moss carpets the path,
fall freshness permeates the air.
October afternoon offers
quiet contemplation
as I walk the river trail.

In the distance, fluttering wings
stir cottonwood leaves.
Ring-tail hawk maneuvers
through trees and soars
into azure sky to freedom.
Rustling in the underbrush
announces arrival of a squirrel.
Sitting tall and motionless,
it observes me with caution;
then quickly scurries to safety.

Struck still by divine power, I see
tiny, blue berries around my feet.
Above, tree branches intertwine
like fingers of lovers holding hands.
Cathedral-like canopy of ashe junipers
steals my breath. Filled with awe,
I embrace this holy moment.

PHENOMENON

Slowly, night overtakes the light of day.
Hovering above the horizon, orange glow
welcomes first display of stars.

An oversized white ball appears,
suspended in air as if by magic.
Close enough to touch,
I stretch my arm.
Sadly, reality overrides the illusion.

Awed by its magnificence,
I search for defining details —
      two dark seas stare at me
      as if a mystery to reveal.
      The guise of a mouth,
      whispering secrets in my ear,
      invites me once more into the fantasy.

The man in the moon, an ancient myth;
but on this night, a whimsical possibility.
I gaze intrigued at the October supermoon.

Another Winter Day

Days are cold and nights even colder since winter arrived.
With blustery winds and icy crystals on blades of dead grass,
each day dawns boldly announcing its weather forecast.

A second cup of coffee, cozy in front of the wood stove,
I read morning meditations and plan the day.
Dreaming dog dreams, Cotton lies beside my feet.

While the wind blows relentlessly sending shivers up my spine,
I feed horses, chip ice in water troughs, and muck stalls.
With chores finished, the warm house offers needed relief.

Sitting at the computer, I look across the wheat field
as ideas, words, sounds, and visions fill my mind.
My fingers touch the keys, the writing begins.

THE FIRST WINTER SNOW

Hush, listen — long-awaited snow begins to fall.
Delicate lacey flakes swish softly through the air,
and a winter night magically transforms.

Moonbeams twinkle in the night sky
daring snow crystals to glisten and glow.
In the cold mist, snowflakes dance to nature's rhythm.

Children turn and twirl amidst the snow flurries.
Wonder fills their faces and joy lights their eyes
when falling flakes touch their tongues with cold.

There is a quiet stillness, as the ground turns white
and icicles sparkle on tree branches.
The world seems to stop for this wintry miracle.

Peacefulness fills the air to remind us —
escape from this chaotic, frenzied world
is found when awed by the first winter snow.

HAIKU

Frozen pastureland
glistens under lunar light —
    coyotes stalk prey

CHRISTMAS EVE

It is Christmas Eve and snow is falling,
the ground's covered in a blanket of white.
The angel voices are softly calling
on this glorious, wondrous, silent night.

The ground's covered in a blanket of white
glistening under the light of the moon.
On this glorious, wondrous, silent night
the world will be a white wonderland soon.

Glistening under the light of the moon,
the angel voices are softly calling.
The world will be a white wonderland soon.
It is Christmas Eve and snow is falling.

A New Year

Resolutions —
that list of hopes and dreams
of this New Year's substitutions
replacing prior year's unsound extremes.
Expectations
perhaps demand more from me.
I must be brave, avoid temptations,
and claim my true, unique authentic self.
Adventure waits for me,
today begins anew.

BLANK PAGES

Another year has come and gone.
Will I shroud myself in struggles and heartaches
or savor the memories of happiness and love?

    The choice is mine.

Pages of one's life are written day by day
often with haste and frustration,
sometimes with ease and longing for more time.

Year after year, images stamped on our hearts
become the narrative of our lives,
shared within the circle of family and friends.

What story will I create during the next 365 days?
Blank pages await the stroke of my pen,
and endless possibilities anticipate my command.

    The choice is mine . . .

HAIKU

Beyond melting snow
lies the sweet promise of spring —
    crocus bloom again

BIRTH OF SPRING

Spring slips tentatively into North Central Texas
pressing purposely against the remnants of winter.
Rain and cold blustery winds resemble fading
images of past wintry days.
New growth pushes unwilling ground to reveal
glorious birth of this season's first display of finery.

HAIKU

Happy tulips bloom
color palette bursting forth —
    winter canvas ends

The Promise of Spring

Spring comes every year with the promise
of garden dreams. When flowers push through deadness,
the ashen color of winter becomes only a memory.
Vibrant colors once again paint our world.

This dynamic energy births my spring dreams.
What will I imagine this year to improve
landscape beds in my yard, to conserve water,
and to provide a sanctuary for birds and butterflies?

Preparing the soil includes weeding and mulching.
Native plants offer best results for growth and
sustainability. Alternative water supplies provide
soaking when needed and conserve other sources.

Plants of red, yellow, and purple coax hummingbirds
and butterflies to the garden. Shade trees offer a place
to perch, rest, and roost for native birds, while various
water features offer needed refreshment for all wildlife.

The list of possibilities is endless. Ideas to protect
the environment and enjoy a beautiful garden
are within my capabilities. The promise of spring
is around the corner. How will my dream come to life?

LADY REDBUD AND HER FOUR DAUGHTERS

The morning sun embraces earth today
as Lady Redbud reaches for the sky.
Her fuchsia gown inflames as sunbeams play
and bounce along each branch from bud to bud.
Across the drive four youthful redbuds sway
in perfect rhythm to the gentle breeze.
Has spring at last arrived and will it stay?
The morning sun embraces earth today.

All day the trees stand tall in proud display
to offer birds a shady home with ease.
The babies chirp while mamas watch and pray
to keep their flock from predators bad blood.

As Lady Redbud reaches for the sky
her daughters raise their branches to obey.
The morning sun embraces earth today.

SONG OF THE MOCKINGBIRD

I hear the song of mockingbird
in early hours of the morn.
Sometimes it is sweet melody,
at times it sounds forlorn.

I hear the calls of mockingbirds
in hours during afternoon.
All playful notes ring loud and clear
as young birds chase and croon.

I hear the sound of mockingbird
in eventide's sweet hours too.
Regardless of the time of day
it always sings on cue.

I hear the trills of mockingbirds;
and yet they sound too much the same
as warbles of the birds near by
that want a song to claim.

I hear the song of mockingbird
all hours of the day and night.
It never stops for quiet rest,
but sings with all its might!

LIFE'S GOOD

Golden stalks of wheat blowin' in the wind, while the fur
on my back ruffles in the breeze and the sun warms my nose,

>as I stretch . . . and yawn.

Over in the pasture Mo and Buddy are grazin'.
I 'member when I'd round those boys up for supper,
but these days they mosey to the barn without much help.

Lying here on the porch, I keep my eye on things.
I might chase a squirrel, maybe two, or rabbits on a good day;
mostly I just watch the one who loves me workin' the place.
We're both gettin' a little slow, do more sittin' than workin'.

Evenin' comes as the sky becomes a pinkish-orange glow,
and another day ends as the full moon begins to rise. Slowly,
he rocks the porch swing back and forth. It gently creaks.

"Cotton, ol' girl," he says, "don't get much better than this."
I cock my ear in agreement . . .

>then stretch . . . and yawn. Life's good!

TAKE FLIGHT

A baby mockingbird alone
in desert willow tree,
not breath nor movement made
to be as still as it could be.

A covering of willow leaves
with blossoms in full bloom
did hide the baby bird
in a cozy, protective womb.

The mother bird seemed far away
perhaps in search of food,
so little bird did what it could
to stay alert and shrewd.

It clutched the limb with toes so tight
and tried to give its all,
but little bird was growing tired
and hoped it would not fall.

It did not sing, or cry, nor bat
its baby eyes, but stayed
upon its perch to wait until
the mama came with aid.

But mama watched her baby bird
from high atop a tree,
and gave her hymn of blessing
as loud as it could be.

"My fledgling dear, please hear my song
and know how proud am I
that you have passed the test today.
Now spread your wings and fly!"

So little bird released its toes
and flapped its wings to rise.
Then soared above the willow tree
into the evening sky.

The moral of this story is
to always hang on tight,
until it's time to spread your wings —
then let yourself take flight.

AWAKEN

As the porch swing gently sways, I sit comfortably still
to witness the North Texas morning come alive.
Though daily temperatures will soar over 100 degrees,
the morning breeze feels almost cool as it caresses my face.

The sun creeps over the horizon to announce the dawn.
Sprinklers water lawns to give a much-needed drink,
and blades of grass appear to raise their heads in thankfulness.
Sunflowers, periwinkles, and begonias bathe in the sunlight.

Cardinals, blue jays, and sparrows dive toward the birdbath,
each hoping to get the first splash of the morning.
Lying by my feet, our dog quietly surveys her surroundings,
as she waits for the first squirrel to make an appearance.

Peace surrounds me. I close my eyes and am filled
with gratitude. My spirit awakens as I sit in the stillness.
I slowly breathe in and out, consciously aware
that a powerful creative energy brings life to me.

A loving power surrounds me with its gentle embrace.
Energized and empowered, I breathe deeply one more time.
A mockingbird's squawk breaks the silence —
I open my eyes and rise to tackle the chores of the day.

The Child Within

Lying in the green grass
enjoying the warmth of the sun,
I gaze deeply into the morning sky.

Various forms and shapes appear,
as clouds come alive.
I contemplate their images.

The sun warms my face,
grass cushions my body.
I close my eyes to block the sun.

I remember past experiences —
friends, parties, dances, first love.
All were important to me.

But age catches up —
youth's pleasures only memories.
Without permission, life moves quickly.

I ponder this passing of time.
The mirror may reveal the truth,
but the child is still within.

Lying in the green grass
enjoying the warmth of the sun,
I gaze deeply into the morning sky.

THANK YOU

In a simple thank you note my granddaughter wrote,
"I love you and Christmas." I laughed.
My heart filled with joy, my eyes with tears.

She had fun that week making Krispie Treats,
playing softball, watching Mary Poppins.
We rode the trails rescuing princesses
and picnicked in the park with the big slide.

Little brother paid no mind. He went about his business,
happy to be outdoors, free to run and explore.
The week was special and much too short as always.

"Thank you in my heart" she ended the note.
I smiled at the simplicity and wisdom of those words.
Soon they will come again to run, play, and explore . . .
each visit bringing treasured memories to share.

Baby

Little black eyes peer over the grass.
Two brown ears still and erect listen —
motionless, baby rabbit waits patiently.

I watch in awe at its natural instinct.
A perceived threat requires stillness,
so baby waits as if frozen in time.

Finally, I slowly and quietly inch closer.
Eyes move, nose twitches;
baby rabbit scampers out of reach to safety.

I smile and go inside to finish the chores of the day.
Little black eyes peer out from under the porch.
Cautiously, baby moves into the soft, green grass.

Displaced

Morning sun rays and water sprays
dance across my back revealing
hues of red, coral, and turquoise.
Fins sparkle aquamarine.

>It is beyond the shores of logic, but I have landed
>in a recycled birdbath turned flowerpot!

Surrounded by pink and white periwinkles,
my body sits on cool, wet dirt.
But as daily temperatures rise,
the dirt bed dries and hardens.

Overheated, I crave clear, blue water.
I dream of freely swimming —
hours on hours in my river habitat,
free to explore and perfect new diving techniques.

Nightly soaking brings both
needed moisture and fading memories.
Cast in potter's clay, I yearn for home —
a fish out of water.

A Dog's Day

In regal pose, paws crossed in front,
she surveys her surroundings. The acres
within her line of sight offer many possibilities.
She contemplates her strategy for the day.

Horses graze in the pasture but
offer no indication of needed supervision.
Barking dogs in the distance raise her ears;
she quickly determines danger is not imminent.

With no squirrels in sight, her head rests on her paws.
The cool morning breeze gently ruffles her fur
and soothes her into a relaxed, peaceful position.
She is content as her eyes slowly close.

After awhile, sounds of laughter arouse her.
Visiting grandchildren shout,
"Cotton, where are you, girl?"
Quickly she runs toward the voices.
Swaddled up in hugs, she offers
her Hollywood dog smile.

"Come on, girl. Let's go exploring!"
Quickly following their lead, she runs ahead
to guide the way. Along the river trails,
the four of them spend the afternoon exploring.

Bugs, flowers, animal droppings, and rocks
hold their attention for most of the afternoon.
Lying under a canopy of trees, Cotton listens
to their voices — school, friends, movies.

While the summer breeze gently rocks
the leaves above their heads, the afternoon lends
itself to a nap. A squawking mockingbird awakens
their sleepy spirits. "Come on, girl, time to go home."

Cotton's playmates shower her with hugs,
and sadly say good-bye. From her place on the porch,
she sighs as they leave. Reclaiming her regal pose,
she surveys her surroundings. Resting her head
on her paws, she is content,
as her eyes . . . slowly . . . close.

TEXAS SUMMER

Another summer day begins —

tall grasses sway, baby birds feed, horses graze
in pastures. The beauty of the Texas morning
disguises the cruelty of the afternoon.

>Daisies raise their heads
>welcoming the morning sun,
>comfort will fade soon.

It's a hot, lazy day. I sit on the porch and
watch sweat beads run down my ice tea glass.
Traffic sounds in the distance
promise travel to a cooler place.

I sip my tea . . .

>afternoon sun burns,
>critters seek shade from grim heat;
>scorched air hangs heavy.

Dusk comes finally, moderate relief
is welcomed. I scan the sky
for hints of needed rain,
but see no promise of showers.

>Colorful sunsets
>adorn Texas evening skies,
>parched land rests at night.

HEAT WAVE

People's attitudes are edgy
as Texas temperatures rise over 100 degrees.
The days of July come to a close.

Overall, it's been a relatively cool season,
until the dog-days of summer appeared.
Not much activity now as energy levels sink.

Lawns, flowers, shrubs, and trees plead
for water as they bow under the heat.
The land cries for a cool, refreshing drink.

Tonight weathermen forecast
possible showers and lower temperatures.
Perhaps, the heat wave is coming to an end.

Sounds of thunder in the distance
suggest much needed rain.
Hope swells as we look toward the skies.

Rebirth

The land is dry, no rain in sight —
it waits for night
to bring relief,
if only brief.

All trees and flowers hang their heads
and grieve the dead —
all beauty gone,
all petals drawn.

White pipe deep drills into the earth,
soon brings rebirth.
As water flows,
all plant life grows.

SWEET SUMMER NIGHT

No longer bothered by activities of the day,
I find relief in the soothing sway of the tree swing.
The scent of lavender floats on the evening breeze
and calms my spirit from encounters with daily stresses.

I listen intently to the nocturnal sounds around me —
crickets chirp, dogs bark, a cat meows,
highway traffic hums in the distance.
Somewhere in the shadows, coyotes howl
as darkness promises possible bounty.

Overhead magnificent full moon hangs motionless;
my mind wanders as I gaze into the heavens.
Is there life lingering beyond what I can see?
Will I ever travel beyond the moon and stars?
I am content to ponder all possibilities.

As the tree swing creaks in relaxing rhythm,
I take one last long look at the sprawling Texas sky —
the man in the moon winks knowingly.
Sweet summer night offers me peaceful pose.

HAIKU

Texas summer eve
rattlesnake coiled to strike —
      lovers' walk disturbed

Genuine Love

Cotton, Border Aussie,
a blue merle coloring.
Her fur, velvet to touch;
that crooked smile, charming.
Her heart, open with love.
Her heart, open with love,
as she passed quietly
looking into our eyes.
No more aging or pain —
but, for us, hearts broken.

CLOSING THOUGHTS

WRITER'S CHOICE

With fingers perched on computer keys,
I contemplate words to fill this page.
Closing my eyes, I breathe deeply and
allow ideas to stream into my consciousness.

Images of love, romance, friendships,
family relationships, celebrations
come alive in my mind's eye.
I consider the possibility of each one.

       What will I write today?

Dreams of success, moments of failure,
and second chances fit together as pieces
of a puzzle to define one's life, or one's faith.
All considered redeeming.

Pages and pages filled with mercy, grace,
and forgiveness overflow book shelves
as authors delve into the mysteries of the Divine.
Still, infinitely more volumes could be written.

       What will I write today?

But wait, world issues of war, hunger,
poverty, financial decline emerge.
Feelings of disbelief, sadness, anger
fuel the hearts of many. All are worthy themes.

What about nature — the beauty of creation,
weather, the changing seasons, or the many
natural wonders of the world? Grand Canyon
or Niagara Falls surely would warrant a page.

        What will I write today?

Numerous topics demand expression
on a piece of paper. The writer — a voice
for the struggles of man, the ills of the world,
and the celebrations of faith and life.

Decisions made every day to explore, enlighten,
and inform. Selections prepared with integrity
to bring value to the reader's life. Alas, the curse
of the writer, always looking for the perfect choice . . .

        perhaps, simplicity is the key.

ABOUT THE AUTHOR

Sheri A. Sutton is an author, devotional writer, and poet. Her newest book, *The Simplicity of Life,* is a book of poems that focus on some ordinary moments in the poet's life that brought joy, laughter, and tears.

As a member of the Wichita Falls Poetry Society and the Poetry Society of Texas, Sutton has been recognized in various local and state contests. Her poetry has been published in her works, *Memorable Moments* and *The One Called Jesus,* as well as the *Wichita Falls Literature and Art Review* and *The Secret Place* magazines, The Poetry Society of Texas' *A Book of the Year, Lifting the Sky, A Celebration of Poetry,* and the *2023 Texas Poetry Calendar.*

Sutton also has published five devotional books, and her devotional writing has been published in *The Secret Place* devotional magazine and the *Lenten Devotions on the Lord's Prayer.* Her work is found as well in the following Advent eBook devotional publications by First Christian Church, Wichita Falls, TX: *Calm and Bright, Chrismons,* and *He Is Called.*

For a limited time, Sutton wrote a monthly newspaper column while serving on the Community Editorial Board of the Times Record News.

Sutton offers professional services that include writing and editing for books, newsletters, and other materials for individuals, companies, or organizations. Fees are competitive within the industry.

In addition, she is available to share her faith and life experiences through public speaking, workshops, Bible studies, or other similar events. For more information, visit her website at www.sheriasutton.com.

Sutton and her husband, Lloyd Mark Sutton, live in Wichita Falls, Texas.

www.ingramcontent.com/pod-product-compliance
Lightning Source LLC
Chambersburg PA
CBHW031505040426
42444CB00007B/1219